Flip close-up WILSON

by JAMES A. HUDSON

SCHOLASTIC BOOK SERVICES
New York Toronto London Auckland Sydney

PHOTO CREDITS
Unless otherwise noted, all photos
courtesy of National Broadcasting Company
DESIGNER: PATRICIA MILLICHAP
Cover Photo: NBC-TV

1st printing .... November 1971
Printed in the U.S.A.

CONTENTS

I. FLIP WILSON, THE "SOCIOLOGIST" 5
II. A COMEDIAN, AGED 6 13
III. CLEROW AND CLARA BARTON 17
IV. EARLY AMBITION 23
V. FLIP AND ORPHAN ANNIE 27
VI. HE GETS PAST BAYONNE 31
VII. A "DRUNK" LAUNCHES HIS CAREER 35
VIII. ON THE ROAD 41
IX. GERALDINE IS "BORN" 45
X. OTHER "ANGELS" APPEAR 51
XI. FLIP'S RISE TO "SUPERSTAR" 55
XII. NO. 1 61
XIII. FLIP AND THE ROLLS ROYCE 65
XIV. THE BOY WHO COULDN'T PLAY
"CHOPSTICKS" 71
XV. FLIP AND THE "IMAGE-MAKERS" 77
XVI. AN EVENING WITH FLIP AND FRIENDS 85

Flip's many faces register a wide range of emotions during his show. But whether he seems surprised, smug, sly, or sad, it's all in fun.

I.

FLIP WILSON, THE "SOCIOLOGIST"

The voice of the master of ceremonies rises into a crescendo as he announces: "And now, ladies and gentlemen—Mr. Flip Wilson!"

From behind the curtain strolls a diminutive (5'-7") man. He stops before the mike and nods his head, to acknowledge the applause. He smiles, but doesn't overdo it. The audience senses that he's completely at ease. Some comedians give you the idea that, for some reason, they've *forced* themselves to come from behind the curtain to stand there and entertain you, as though they're trying to prove something to themselves. They give themselves away by bowing a little too deeply or grinning a little too much.

Not Flip. He just stands there, smiling nicely, confidently, waiting for the applause to die down. The audience regards him as an easy-going, long-time friend. He's not some nervous stranger who's going to try to be funny and maybe fail—causing himself, and the audience, embarrassment. Just by standing there, Flip has many of these people lean-

Obviously it's Flip, not "Geraldine"—but when he makes this gesture, Flip invariably **sounds** like Geraldine. And fans can almost "see" her.

ing forward expectantly. They somehow sense that this cool, collected, yet friendly fellow is going to be amusing, whether or not they've "caught" his act before. And this is obviously the past we're talking about, for these days who *hasn't* caught Flip's act? Then suddenly, Flip double-crosses his eager "friends" with his very first words. He says, "When I was back there, thinking about what I'd do out here, I asked myself if I should do any racial material." He pauses. Some in the predominantly white audience stir uneasily. They aren't sure that this is what they've come to hear. Racial material? Racial material can be quite unfunny. And sometimes it can be embarrassing. Flip's not going to embarrass this white audience by reminding them of past and present sins, is he? Or *is* he? They've come here to laugh, to forget their problems, and the world's problems, too. But here Flip is, threatening to be unfunny and maybe embarrass them.

So, the audience hangs on. Flip hasn't turned them off—yet. But he just might.

While all this is running rapidly through various minds of those seated before him, Flip pauses just long enough to let the full effect of this threat sink in. Then he goes on, "So I decided, why not? Why should I hesitate to express *my* opinion about the racial problem? Why shouldn't I say to you: 'Ladies and gentlemen, we've got to do something about the Indians!'"

Laughter explodes all over the place. It's the kind of full-throated laughter that accompanies great relief. There's a touch of hysteria in it. It says, in effect, "Oh, THAT'S what you mean by 'racial.' THEY'RE who you're talking about. The *Indians*!" Their friend, Flip, is one of them again. Flip stands there deadpan. He hasn't even *heard* the laughter, he's so lost in thought. Or so he makes it appear. There's a slight scowl on his face, as though he's thinking about how to approach the sociological problem which he's raised for serious discussion. As well he might, of course, since the place of the American Indian in society today *is* a problem. Still laughing, the audience waits for Flip's "solution."

"There are some who say the Indians aren't ready yet," reports Flip, the "sociologist." And already the next wave of laughter begins to swell.

"Now some say that's a pretty harsh statement," admits Flip, overriding the laughter. "But it depends on how you look at it. Let's ask ourselves questions like, 'How would you like to build a $50,000 home and have some guy put a wigwam next to it?'"

The salvo of laughter that greets this line is even louder than the first. Flip has now stepped into another dimension. A moment ago, he'd indicated somewhat absurdly that he was a "moderate" on the Indian question. But now, the reasoning behind his "prejudice" against Indians is just too "far-out." Even Indians don't live in wigwams anymore, do they? And the idea of such an unreconstructed red man even *wanting* to pitch his tent in a "lily white" suburb is just too much.

Flip has carried out his initial threat by delving into racial material, all right. And, in doing so, he's mirrored attitudes still held by many white people. But it's a crazy looking glass he holds up to the audience. In it they see not themselves, but they can make out the comically distorted images of many others they know. It's like looking into a mirror

8

at an amusement-park funhouse.

Flip Wilson carries his own "funhouse" with him. He quickly proves to the audience that he doesn't have a one-track mind—or just one "funhouse" mirror, either. That's enough of this racial stuff, he seems to say. We're all together. We're all here for laughs. In a few minutes, then, he does another trick. Like Alice in Wonderland, he steps right through the magic looking glass. Like Alice, too, he finds a wondrous never-never land on the other side.

Suddenly, for instance, Flip's in 15th-century Spain. Playing all parts, he imagines the scene: Christopher Columbus is trying to persuade Queen Isabella to finance his voyage to America. The queen doesn't seem so sure she should hock all her jewels to back Chris' venture until he mentions that, unless he discovers America, there will be no Ray Charles.

Isabella quickly agrees to the venture. She goes running through her castle shouting with glee: "Chris gone *find* Ray Charles!" As with all women who "appear" in Flip's routines, Isabella speaks in a high-pitched voice that sounds like an under-educated but lively black woman from the deep south. "Chris gone *find* Ray Charles," Isabella squeals with delight. "He gone America on that boat. What you say!"

The audience howls.

Where and when did the above scene take place? At no place in particular, yet in many places. It's a montage of scenes that happened in Boston, San Francisco, Chicago, New York, and many places in

9

Flip, singer Glen Campbell, and the Supremes.

between. Scenes similar to this one, comprised of the distinctive Flip Wilson brand of humor, were taking place in small clubs years before he became known to millions as a big television star.

Flip Wilson has been "around" a long time. It just took television a long time to catch up with him. Perhaps TV wasn't "ready" for Flip Wilson. But all that is past history. In 1965, he "arrived" on network television in a guest appearance on Johnny Carson's *Tonight Show*. Since then, a fitting musical theme for his rapid rise to stardom would be "Up, Up and Away." In just five short years—as almost anyone within reach of a TV set or newspaper knows—Flip had his own weekly network program.

Flip and the Gospel Singers, "regulars" on his show.

Though Flip Wilson, the comedian, has become so famous, relatively few TV viewers know much about Flip Wilson, the man. Their lack of knowledge is understandable. Many of those who work on Flip's show know little about him, either. He's one of the most private men who've earned star status in Hollywood, a town noted for its publicity-seekers. This is the story of a man who, while he's seldom actively sought publicity, has received reams of it—yet whose complete biography remains tantalizingly elusive. It's a "success story" beyond the grasp of most dreams.

Above all, it's the story of a man dedicated to a serious art—the art of comedy.

They may not exactly be birds of a feather, but when Sesame Street's "Big B appeared on Flip's show, the unusual team made a big hit.

II.

A COMEDIAN, AGED 6

Flip's long road to success, which recently has appeared to be a high-speed superhighway, began as a narrow, rubble-strewn alleyway in the slums of Jersey City, N.J. One thing most slums always seem to have plenty of is kids. Jersey City's was no exception. If Flip ever had trouble finding other kids to play with, he could always play with his brothers and sisters. He had 17, all told.

Slum families are often unhappy ones, and to find a happy slum family with 18 kids is, for all practical purposes, impossible. Flip's family was no exception to this rule, either. When Flip was 8 years old, his mother and father separated, with various Wilson children being farmed out to several foster homes.

Under these conditions, many children would lose much of whatever self-confidence they'd managed to cultivate. Certainly, almost any child subjected to Flip's early experiences might lose some faith in himself. Flip was shunted from one foster

"Boy, you should have seen the one that got away!" During an off-camera break, Flip makes a gesture that could be used in a big fish story.

home to another. He confessed to me years later that, in one home, he was so miserable he asked to be sent to reform school instead. Eventually he got his wish. Yet none of these traumas seemed to diminish a conviction the boy had that in the long run things would turn out all right. It was a remarkable conviction, unshaken even when his mother abandoned him. In trying to explain it, Flip says, "I always felt that I had a guardian angel."

14

A real-life "guardian angel" or two to ease the way somewhat would crop up much later in Flip's life. But the road of his first few years was, indeed, rocky, and the remarkable thing is that Flip held onto this stubborn faith long enough to see it realized.

One might wonder if something that Flip and his friends had discovered a couple of years before the Wilson family broke up didn't have some bearing on that remarkable faith. Flip, who was born on December 8, 1933, had started going to school when he was six; and it was shortly after then that he and his playmates had made this discovery. They found that many kids, when they first start school, are shy and withdrawn. The idea of standing before their classmates and reciting aloud or acting in a play terrifies them and sends them into a state of tongue-tied shock. Not so with Flip.

He was so outgoing and gregarious that the teacher chose him to lead the class in the daily Pledge of Allegiance to the flag. Flip welcomed this chore, since it gave him a chance to show his audience a few of his tricks. Flip was a classroom "cut-up." More than thirty years later, some of his former schoolmates still remember how Flip was always coming up with "new material"—songs and funny poems to recite while waiting for the remainder of the class to assemble to recite the daily Pledge.

Incidentally, his "billing" for these early "acts" didn't list him as Flip Wilson. For the first 16 years of his life he labored under his given name, Clerow Wilson. "I don't know why they hung that name on me," Flip told me with a grin. "I was never too crazy about it."

Rolling merrily along, Flip gags it up with oversized tricycle. Off-stage, his favorite vehicle is a blue Rolls Royce. With four wheels.

His first dramatic role was easy.
"I played a wounded soldier.
My part was just to lie there!"

III.

CLEROW AND CLARA BARTON

Though Clerow felt comfortable playing before a live audience at the age of six—and we can believe that "comfortable" is an understatement—he gave no thought to making the stage his career until years later. Three years later, to be precise, when Flip was nine. Meanwhile, something had happened to whet his appetite for being an entertainer. It was a school play, starring "Clara Barton."

"Clara Barton" was Flip's first appearance on a real stage. His previous antics, as well as his serious recitations of the Pledge of Allegiance, had been performed merely by standing in front of the class. But a real stage! The thought must have been a trifle frightening, even for such an "old pro" as nine-year-old Flip. It's probably safe to assume, however, that the prospect of appearing on stage brought Flip a feeling sweeter than fear: He must have been happily excited, too.

But a "fly" soon landed in Flip's "soup." "Clara Barton," of course, would *star* in the production; so

A "friendly" game of cards with Bill Cosby in a skit on one of Flip's shows taught Flip the virtue of maintaining a "poker face." (Bill won.)

our hero could hardly expect to get "top billing." But it did seem that, for a boy of Flip's talents, they could have found a little more imaginative role than the one assigned to him. "I was given the part of a wounded soldier," Flip says with a grin. "My part was just to lie there."

A bit part of such limitations would be difficult for any but the most stage-frightened to embrace with great enthusiasm. But to a boy who was far from stage-frightened—who, indeed, was used to being the "star" of his own classroom "show"— such a bit role was particularly vexing.

Day after day, Flip lay on the stage during rehearsal, "playing" the wounded soldier. Considering a mind as restless as Flip's, it's more than a little conceivable that he thought about how he could

18

Maybe everyone doesn't find a broken leg so funny. But when Cosby visited "patient" during a skit, both "broke up" themselves.

"dress up" his small role. Should he groan a little louder? Should he stagger to his feet again and, finally, collapse on his back with outstretched arms?

But, apparently, no possibility that was aesthetically satisfying occurred to the young thespian. So he just lay there during those long rehearsals, memorizing everyone's lines to pass the time.

When the big moment arrived, for which all the young actors had been working so hard—all, maybe, but Flip—a crisis arose that would have been worthy of Broadway: The "star" couldn't make the curtain call.

Some accounts of this historic event have offered the explanation that "Clara Barton" suddenly suffered an acute attack of a "disease" to which Flip was happily immune—stage fright. Flip was more

19

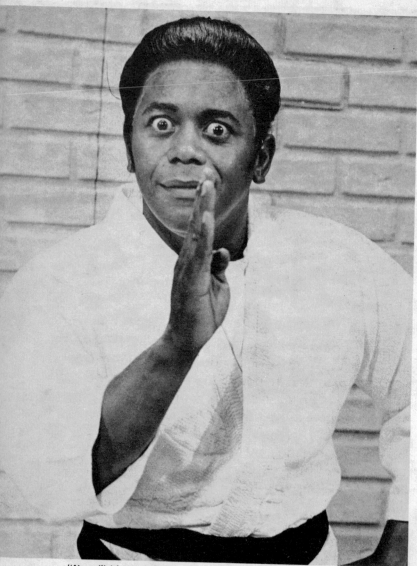

"Ah, so!" It's the karate expert himself, complete with Oriental wig and a black belt testifying to his prowess. Note the frightening gaze!

charitable in his version of the story. "I think she was sick or something," he said. "I don't know. It's been so long ago."

Whatever the cause of the crisis, the play's director was thrown into the classic state of panic traditionally associated with such theatrical moments. He went rushing around, looking for a last-minute substitute for the stricken "Clara." Alas, the "star" had appeared so confident in her role—during rehearsals, at least—that she'd been assigned no understudy. And, after polling members of the cast, the director discovered, to his great dismay, that Flip was the only one who just happened to have memorized Clara's lines.

The director then made an agonizing—and, it should be noted, *brave*—decision. In the best tradition of "the show must go on," he stuck a blonde wig on Flip, shod him in high-button shoes, and— behold!—there was his new Clara Barton!

As far as anyone seems to remember, Flip went through the performance flawlessly.

Flip was asked once if his role of "Clara" also had been the stage debut of "Geraldine," the comic female character Flip has made so famous. Had Flip spoken Clara's lines in a boyish falsetto?

"No," he said, smiling. "Just playing Clara was good enough at the time, so I used my own voice."

Obviously, when necessary, Flip can play a straight dramatic role.

But during some moment of that play, Flip—in blonde wig and high-button shoes—must have decided to pursue an entertainment career. Right?

Wrong.

Flip said that decision came at another time.

Flip says he spent years learning to appear "effortless." He obviously succeeded. Here's how relaxed he can seem during an act seen by millions.

Surrounded by laughter,
Flip made a serious decision.

IV.

EARLY AMBITION

It was an unusual place to make a serious decision. The Mosque Theater was jumping with laughter; and it appeared doubtful that a single serious thought could survive in the place.

Yet one person sitting in the audience, the nine-year-old boy named Clerow Wilson, was arriving at a decision that not only would change the course of his life but would eventually have an impact on millions of other people.

Small for his age, he had no trouble curling up in his seat in the darkened theater as he watched the vaudeville actors go through their slapstick routines before the bright footlights. The year was 1942, long before television had dealt the death-stroke to vaudeville as popular entertainment; and this scene in Jersey City was being duplicated in hundreds of theaters throughout the land. Visual entertainment couldn't be had then by the flick of a switch at home. TV was still confined to experimentation and had not yet marched into living rooms to take up occupancy as a permanent house guest.

In 1942, you still had to work a bit to find visual entertainment. At home, you had the radio, of course. And kids from affluent families could consider themselves lucky if they owned their own set. But even radios weren't as plentiful as they were later to become when technology, by the development of inexpensive transistors, spawned millions of cheap sets. Old-fashioned radio sets were still expensive; and most kids—certainly those brought up in Flip's neighborhood—were happy when their turn came to choose a favorite program on the family radio. Huddled around the "wireless," they'd follow the adventures of such heroes as the Shadow, the Green Hornet, and Boston Blackie, or listen to the spookiest program of them all—*Inner Sanctum*.

Like any kid his age, Clerow also had his cache of comic books at home, and he kept abreast of developments in the comic strips of daily newspapers. But in 1942 many kids had learned to take such amusements as the radio and "the funnies" more or less for granted. The best entertainment of all was still "the picture show." And it was a rare and unfortunate youth who, during the week, couldn't somehow earn, borrow, or "snitch" the 25 cents necessary for the price of admission to most "neighborhood houses." Even the kids who found themselves short of funds when Saturday afternoon arrived were likely to congregate under the theater marquees in the hope of catching a ticket-taker off guard. Sneaking in sometimes was half the fun.

But such problems of finance and logistics were far from young Flip's mind at the moment. As the audience howled at the vaudevillians' on-stage antics, he could congratulate himself for being one of the lucky ones. It was enough to make a nine-year-old boy want to hug his knees to his chest in sheer delight. Today, it wasn't just a movie, either. Today, it was vaudeville, man. And it wasn't just another group of comics trying out those old wheezers that Flip already knew by heart. These "cats" had really fresh material.

So Flip sat there clutching his sides with laughter and making this serious decision. He probably didn't *look* serious. His schoolmates recall that his face, even then, was strikingly mobile. One moment it would seem to be that of a delighted cherub. The next, he might look like an imp or a pixie. In his smile was a great deal of dazzlingly white and beautifully even teeth; all in all, hardly the face of one you'd suspect of making a solemn vow to himself. But, as Flip described the scene, that's how it was when, in the semidarkness of the Old Mosque Theater in Jersey City, he decided to make his career as a comedian.

"I'm not even exactly sure who the comedians were that time," he said. "I believe the act was called Stump and Stumpy. But, anyway, that was it. I knew then that I had to make people laugh, too."

Relaxed himself in front of TV cameras, Flip enables his guests to relax, too—even if it means holding their hands, as here he does with Lola Falana. She doesn't seem to mind. Neither does Flip.

V.

FLIP AND ORPHAN ANNIE

The year that Flip Wilson decided to become a comedian—1942—was a bad year for laughs. In December of the previous year, Japanese military forces had staged the sneak attack on Pearl Harbor that plunged the United States into World War II. In less than three months, Gen. Douglas MacArthur's forces had been forced to retreat to Australia; most Americans wanted desperately to believe the general when he vowed, "I shall return." But many had their private fears and doubts. At best, the U.S. was caught in a war which seemed endless and for which it was ill-equipped. Americans tried hard, but many of them had little to laugh about.

To boys of Flip's age, World War II was an event taking place in faraway lands, mainly among those who made up the mysterious world of adults. But Flip already knew one kind of warfare. He was in a very real battle for survival himself.

As Flip sat talking in his manager's office, the scenes of Clerow Wilson's boyhood seemed, in the most obvious sense, quite distant both in time and place. From the windows of this office, tastefully furnished with modern furniture and orange plaid drapery, you look out upon the white stone and gleaming glass windows of a well-kept office building. In the street below, the pavement is alive with traffic—yellow taxis, green buses, and varicolored cars, some of them chauffeur-driven limousines. Occasionally Flip's soft voice would lower; his eyes, capable of rolling like marbles during a comic routine, would diminish in a distant gaze. For the moment, Flip wasn't on 57th Street in upper-midtown Manhattan but back in the impoverished haunts he knew as a boy in Jersey City.

One of the first questions brought on that deeply reflective look: "Flip, I understand you came from a very large family. How many brothers and sisters did you have?"

Then came the look, the quiet voice. "Yes, I came from a very large family. There were 18 of us kids— nine boys and nine girls. I was the tenth child."

He described his old neighborhood: "You could call it a poverty area. That sounds nicer than 'slum area.' But that's what it was."

What had been his father's occupation? "He was a carpenter and handyman." Flip paused. Then, with just a trace of a smile: "He was a creator. He made things—like all us kids." Again the distant look.

Had he been a good student, despite the odds? It must not be easy to do homework with so much distraction around. "Yes," said Flip, "I was a very good student. I liked English and history. And I was always a big comic-book reader. I liked listening to

28

the radio, too, to all those old radio serials. I was always ready to go on a trip of fantasy. My favorite comic-strip characters were Bugs Bunny, Captain Marvel, and Little Orphan Annie. I could never finish a whole episode of Annie, though. I must have felt some sort of identification with her. When things got too bad for her, I'd just split the scene. I'd wait until she'd been rescued, then I'd start reading her again."

Flip's face remained perfectly serious and his voice was still distant as he confessed the boyhood "crush" he'd had on Little Orphan Annie. When kids are thoroughly unhappy, they have two major routes to escape their troubles. They can physically run away, or they can stage a mental retreat by amusing themselves with their own thoughts.

Young Clerow tried both escape routes. The "trips of fantasy" he'd mentioned weren't quite enough to insulate him from unhappiness. He was so miserable at one foster home that he asked if he couldn't rejoin one of his older brothers. That would have meant going to the reform school to which the brother had been sentenced. "After I ran away eight times, they sent me there" (to the reformatory), he recalled.

"The first nice people I ever met were in that school. This teacher took an interest in me. In fact, he gave me the first birthday presents I ever got—a box of Crackerjacks and a can of ABC shoe polish.

"Altogether, I ran away from home thirteen times. But I could never get farther than Bayonne."

29

Former heavyweight champion Muhammed Ali (Cassius Clay) seems amused as comic champ Wilson verbally spars with him. It was a close "decision"—thanks to Flip's writers, and Ali's poise. But some fans were "KO'ed."

VI.

HE GETS PAST BAYONNE

By the time he was 16, Flip was willing to try almost any means of getting out of the slums of Jersey City. He'd been placed in a total of three foster homes, and none of them had made him feel as though he belonged there. After his release from reform school, he'd briefly tried living with his father, who was then working as a janitor. And that hadn't worked, either. He wanted very much to continue his education, so he'd gone back to school. But that, too, as far as he was concerned, had been just another failure. Why? Because, for one thing, he was always broke. Another reason was that he never felt comfortable in his threadbare clothes. Finally, the whole situation became too much to bear. Flip took a step which many youths would consider sheer desperation. "I fudged my age to 17, so I could get into the Air Force," he said. "I was sent to Lackland, Texas, Hamilton Field, and then to Guam."

As far as Flip was concerned, any of these places was better than his old neighborhood in Jersey City.

"The Air Force beat parking cars for a living," he said. Besides, the Air Force gave its men a certain amount of spending money. Though this didn't mean that Flip still wasn't "financially embarrassed" on occasion, he had a new, sharply pressed uniform on his back and new, highly polished shoes on his feet. Secure in the knowledge that he appeared as presentable as any of his newly made friends in the Air Force, Flip soared in spirit and quickly established a reputation as a barracks-room clown. It was during this period of his life that he acquired the nickname by which the world now knows him.

How did he get the name "Flip"?

"Well, I was always saying and doing things that made them think I'd flipped, I guess. Or maybe, if it was a pretty good line I pulled, they thought they were going to flip. Anyway, my name became 'Flip.' And it's been that ever since."

Flip now had new clothes, a comfortable place to sleep, three square meals a day, pocket money, and congenial companions. But fortune continued smiling on him, and soon there arrived at the scene one of those "guardian angels" who Flip had always felt would arrive. For an angel, he was in an unusual guise—the military uniform of Flip's commanding officer.

Flip's C.O. singled him out as a young airman who deserved special attention. For one thing, the officer obviously didn't think the youthful barracks-room clown took himself seriously enough. "His name was Lancaster," Flip said. "He was real good to me. He told me I had to go to school and learn more English and learn how to type. Well, I began goofing off the first time. He caught me going into San Francisco with the fellows instead of going to school. No, he didn't get too mad. But the next time, he gave me a round-trip ticket on the bus instead of the money. So I didn't goof off any more."

Flip proved himself worthy of the C.O.'s unusual kindness, which certainly went beyond the call of duty. But something else should also be noted.

"Did you say your commanding officer was white, and from the South?" Flip was asked.

"That's right," he said. "There was never any trouble. He seemed to like me, and that was it."

Flip's extracurricular training while in the Air Force turned out to be quite valuable, especially the typing lessons. Eventually, he'd use this skill to type out his routines as well as write a book on which he's still working. But the C.O. did Flip an even bigger favor! He decided that Flip's talents while clowning around in the barracks far outshone his abilities as an Air Force clerk. By pulling a few official strings, the C.O. had Flip transferred to the Air Force's entertainment section. This gave Flip his first experience as a "professional" comedian.

An "arresting performance" was given by Zero Mostel, shown here with an unlikely looking police officer. Flip seems undecided whether to "run in" the zany suspect—or to run away from him.

VII.

A "DRUNK"
LAUNCHES HIS CAREER

When Flip Wilson was in the Air Force, for the first time in his life "the breaks" started falling his way. North Korean troops had invaded South Korea, and the United States was involved in another war. But, instead of being sent to Korea with thousands of other airmen, Flip was assigned the pleasant duty of entertaining lonely servicemen, many of them en route to the war.

Flip's comic routines, at this point in his budding career, were simple compared to the standards he sets today. It's doubtful he could have indulged in much social satire, bound in by military "regs" as he was. But it's just as doubtful that he'd have done so, regardless of what stage he'd been given. The world might not have been ready for Flip Wilson during the four years he spent in the Air Force. That's the kind way of looking at it; for there's also no reason to believe that he was ready to entertain vast, mature audiences either. As he himself has said, "It takes about 15 years of working at it to develop into a good comedian."

When Louis ("Satchmo") Armstrong appeared on Flip's show, he seemed to "dig" his host's sense of humor as much as Flip enjoyed "Pop's" singing and trumpet playing. Flip mourned the death of this great musician.

This doesn't mean that Flip wasn't a resounding success with his built-in audiences of servicemen of his own age. Perhaps bored even more than he was by service life, they laughed uproariously at his "lectures" on such zany but cornball subjects as "The Sex Habits of the Coconut Crab." And this experience was undoubtedly priceless as far as Flip's career was concerned. Where else but in the armed services could he have been able to serve an apprenticeship as a comedian while playing before such ready-made and enthusiastic audiences? The heavy sound of the applause he got must have been unforgettable to the young entertainer. It just might have done two things: It might bolster his self-confidence and cause him to be more resolved than ever to succeed at his craft in civilian life; and it might also be likely to increase whatever impatience he might feel while working toward that success.

But Flip had more persistence than impatience—and it was a good thing, for he had need of it. He started needing it as soon as he received his honorable discharge from service in 1954. He immediately discovered that there was no demand in the marketplace for a 20-year-old comic who lectured on such subjects as the love life of coconut crabs. He considered the want ads and then applied for a job—as a bellhop.

Luck strikes in strange places. A job as a $40-a-week bellhop at the Manor Plaza Hotel in San Francisco might not have appeared to offer glowing prospects for immediate advancement in the world. Considering all the circumstances, Flip could have done a lot worse. He could have been "parking cars in Jersey City," for example. The labor market was glutted with returning servicemen in 1954, and almost any job was hard to find. What's more, his job as bellhop offered him a rare opportunity, one not likely to be found on a Jersey City parking lot. Flip was bright enough to see the opportunity—and brash enough to seize it.

Hotels furnish numerous funny situations, such as mixed-up luggage, lost keys, forgotten room numbers, and mistaken identities. But Flip did not

Singer Bing Crosby, an addicted golfing "nut" in real life, gave Flip a few pointers on the game when he appeared as a guest. Judging from Flip's "body English," it appears that he could use a few more lessons.

spend much time in studying them for their comic possibilities. "Nothing really happened until that time I got into the hotel act," he said.

Instead of wasting time elsewhere, Flip had spent as much time as he could concentrating on the hotel's floor show. "There was a dance group rehearsing," he said, "for an act that was going to play at the hotel. The act was supposed to be set in a bar. But there was a lull in the show, and I suggested to the director that he should have a 'drunk' do a walk-on part at that point, to liven things up." The lull Flip referred to was a brief pause in the show while the dancers changed costumes.

"Well," Flip continued, "after I made the suggestion, the director said, 'Well, try it.' So I did, and he liked it and said, 'Say something.' So I started ad-libbing, and I guess I kind of stopped the show."

Again, Flip had made a big hit with an audience. But he still was to learn the hard way—by sometimes painful experience—what is meant by "the ladder of success." In few professions can an ambitious aspirant skyrocket to the top, an "overnight discovery." In most cases, as in Flip's, before the top is reached there's a great deal of slow ladder-climbing to do—rung by difficult rung.

But now Flip had achieved the second rung. After learning to entertain his fellow servicemen, he'd begun to learn to amuse older, civilian audiences. But doing a "drunk act," even when it gave him a chance to deliver a number of lines, wasn't enough.

The third rung now had to be climbed.

How did he do it? "Well, next," said Flip, "I hit the road, drifting around the country, looking for other places to work as a comedian."

To play various characters, Flip dons costumes ranging from traditional tuxedo to a carnival barker's straw "boater." But no matter what hat—if any—he wears, Flip's real business is to cause laughter.

"Many of them, when we'd get where we were going, gave me two or three dollars."

VIII.

ON THE ROAD

When an aspiring comedian begins looking for work, he's often embarked on one of the most difficult job-hunts of all. There are no comedy colleges. The job-seeker can't walk into a place, show them his degree as a comedy graduate, and hope to be ushered to the personnel manager to fill out a job application.

When he first began looking for a job of this sort, what experience could Flip cite to persuade club managers to give him a chance? Guam was a long way even from San Francisco, and it didn't get any closer the farther eastward he traveled. Even a club owner in Altoona, Pa., wouldn't be apt to be overwhelmed by the fact that the applicant's latest critical acclaim had been won as an ersatz "drunk" in an act thousands of miles away.

To get a job as a comedian, Flip first had to prove that he was funny. But what if the fellow he was trying to persuade to hire him was too busy to listen? Suppose during a tryout every time he got to a punch line, someone knocked on the door or the phone rang? Or suppose he'd made a good impression on a club manager—but the latter had just hired a comedian. "Come back in a couple of weeks," he might say. Fine. Meanwhile, what was Flip supposed to do to stay alive? There was only a certain number of places that employed comedians in any given town and if Flip struck out at them, there was only one thing to do: Pick up his bag and move on to the next town. There were times during this trying period when Flip went hungry.

"When I was hitchhiking," he said, "I'd get to talking to the people who'd picked me up, and they'd say, 'You'd kill 'em in Denver,' or 'You'd knock 'em dead in Kansas City.' So I just traveled around like that, looking for work and meeting a lot of nice people. I'd try to make their time enjoyable. And many of them, when we'd get where we were going, gave me two or three dollars."

One of Flip's talents as a comedian is an ability to exaggerate. When he talks about his real-life experiences, however, he often speaks in understatement. Sometimes "traveling around" meant playing in a tiny, smoke-filled club for so little money he'd have to pass the hat to buy food. Sometimes it meant sleeping in paper-strewn bus stations or atop parked cars.

Such a life is enough to discourage all but the most determined—and talented—comedians. Most who try to graduate from this tough "school" end up by going back to work behind a lunch counter, take up careers as door-to-door salesmen, or grab whatever other chance they have to "retire" from the field. For every comedian who "makes it" even

"Geraldine," in rare relaxed moment, doesn't quite seem "herself."

in a modest way, there are scores who discover that the life of a struggling young comedian just isn't for them.

But whatever hardship this kind of life dished out to him, Flip was determined to take it—just as he was determined to "make it." He pursued his goal, no matter what the setbacks; he labored at his craft— polishing his lines, perfecting his timing, learning to deal with the occasional heckler, acquiring the ability to "project" poise at all times. And, above all, during this period of learning to turn his trade into an art, he diligently gave free rein to his imagination.

One time while he was doing this, the character Geraldine was "born."

Blowing a kiss to audience, left, "Geraldine" can be sentimental—but seldom is shy. However, other infrequent poses show "her" in various stages of demureness —if you can believe it. (She can be **loud,** too!)

"Play on the harp, Little David!
...What you say!"

IX.

GERALDINE IS "BORN"

One day as Flip was passing through a Midwestern "tank town," he saw a black soldier returning home. The soldier's teenage sister sighted the neighborhood hero from a window of their house and announced the news by calling, "Here come Willie back from the war, Mama. Show Mama how you can march, Willie. Hup, two, three, four!"

The scene made an unforgettable impression on Flip. Soon he was incorporating his version of the girl's high-pitched voice in his comedy routines. Later, in Flip's flipped-out version of history, the voice would be that of the Biblical "fan," Bathsheba, who urges on the "jazz musician," King David, by crying, "Play on the harp, Little David! Play on that harp, honey. What you say!" In another routine, the voice became that of "Queen Isabella Johnson," Christopher Columbus' benefactor; and, still later, the same voice was embodied in Flip's TV character, Geraldine.

This gradual evolution of Geraldine is the most

"Geraldine" is never at a loss for words—and usually is prepared to cope with any emergency. Here "she" whips out a can of hair spray just when Tony Randall's locks might have needed it . . .

graphic illustration of how Flip's comic mind works. Again and again it returns to a theme or a character, seldom if ever to repeat but to refurbish it to suit his changing moods and insights. Sometimes he'll play around with an idea for years before it emerges in final shape.

"For instance," he said, "my Columbus story" (as it was finally recorded on one of Flip's LP records) "takes only seven minutes to tell, but I spent three years polishing it."

Flip is philosophical when speaking about his

46

... and here "Geraldine" seems to expect something in return. The man's obviously not interested. He may be a rare one. Males usually fall for Geraldine's blandishments. She seems to **think** so, anyway!

lean days as an aspiring comedian. "Hungry guys make the best prizefighters and comedians," he said. "But a prizefighter only has to knock out one guy at a time. A comedian has to knock out an entire audience." Here he betrayed an attitude which some may find strange. Long after he's attained a fortune from his talent, Flip Wilson still believes that for comedy to be at its best, it must be the result of hard work. As a direct corollary of this belief, to Flip comedy is obviously a serious subject. He seldom jokes about it. He's forever trying to discover new secrets of just what makes a particular thing funny—and what would make it funnier.

His analytical approach to humor dates back to the time when Flip discovered that there was no short cut to becoming a successful comedian. He would have to discover the "rules" for himself. As far as he was concerned, he'd chosen such an exacting occupation that it would take longer to reach professional competence at it than it does to become a successful lawyer or a brain surgeon. He set himself a goal of 15 years.

"When I was starting out, there was no place for me to go to learn what is funny and how to present the material. So I read everything I could about comedy. I found out that most comics agree it takes fifteen years to learn the trade. They're right! It takes that long because comedy involves so much psychology and being able to speak on all kinds of subjects. You've got to read, learn, educate yourself."

One book which Flip did find somewhat useful was Max Eastman's *The Enjoyment of Humor*. But this work mainly inspired him to start cataloguing his own set of "laws" in a "book of comedy" which he began writing. The fact that he's still working on this manuscript is a mark of how earnest he is about comedy. "I don't think I'm enough of an authority to publish it now," he said. "I have years and years ahead of me. I'm still compiling notes."

Flip concedes that someday, perhaps, his book may help some comedic fledgling avoid some of the difficulties and pitfalls that he has had to overcome. Meanwhile, however, the "rules" he's spelled out mainly serve as guidelines when he's working on his own routines. "In comedy," he says, "there are established ingredients, just as there are in writing a serious play. When I write a piece of material, I check every word of every idea against my notebook. If the material doesn't conform to my rules, I change it."

Flip has read the Eastman book many times and frequently quotes from it. "I always try to keep in mind one law of humor I found in the Eastman book," he said. " 'Things can be funny only when we are in fun.' "

"In the beginning," said Flip, "I analyzed the great comics to find out what made them great. With Bob Hope, it was his timing. With Rochester, his voice. I try to bring out these qualities in myself, along with what I have myself. The basic thing is to be effortless. George Burns is effortless."

Few comedians seem to agree with Flip that comedy requires such analytical treatment. But how many of them can argue with his success? For Flip, anyway, the "Wilson method" obviously works. "No one else that I've run into feels that the depth that I go into is necessary," Flip admitted. "But I feel that just having the natural ability is not enough."

Flip obviously has that natural ability—and has had it all his life. But even after five years of hard "roadwork," training for comedy's "big league," he still was in "the minors."

Singer Perry Como, playing a psychiatrist in a skit with Flip, listens to "Geraldine's" problems—but obviously thinks things could be worse!

X.

OTHER "ANGELS" APPEAR

In 1959, Flip's search for work had taken him to
Miami, Florida, where another "guardian angel"
appeared. This "angel" was a Miami businessman
who saw Flip's act in a small club and realized that
the young comedian had talent and needed money.
This benefactor offered to ease Flip's financial pres-
sures by sending him $50 a week for a year.

Flip gratefully accepted the offer. He's long since
repaid the man, who remains anonymous; but Flip
still remembers the kindness of this "angel" who
helped him out in time of need.

From Miami, Flip went to New York City, where
he became a regular star at the Apollo Theater, in
Harlem. Finally, he was making good money, and
he was performing before audiences far larger than
those to which he'd become accustomed. The Apollo had long been considered tops as far as the Negro
entertainment circuit was concerned. It was still an
extremely long "jump" from 125th Street, in vir-
tually all-black Harlem, to the vast and largely white

audiences that could be commanded from a TV studio "downtown" in Rockefeller Center. But still another "angel" appeared and made this spectacular step possible.

This "angel" was Redd Fox, a veteran Negro comedian who had also starred at the Apollo and had been graduated to such major platforms as Johnny Carson's *Tonight Show*, on which he had appeared as a guest. During one of these appearances, Fox told Carson about a fresh young comedian who, he said, should make a big hit on Carson's program. When a comedian praises another comedian, most talent scouts listen. Carson was all ears; and in August 1965 Flip made his first appearance as a guest on Carson's show. It wouldn't be his last. He quickly had the audience almost crying with laughter with his Christopher Columbus routine. When he put his hand on his hip *a la Geraldine* and gleefully shrieked, "Chris gone *find* Ray Charles!" Carson almost fell off his chair.

Following that happy debut, Flip was a frequent guest on *The Tonight Show*, and later in his career he sometimes "subbed" for the regular host when Carson was vacationing. Ed Sullivan also liked Carson's "discovery" and quickly signed Flip to a contract to appear on his "she-e-w." Flip was a big hit with that audience, too. For the next two seasons he became a familiar and favorite guest on such TV programs as the *Merv Griffin*, the *Joey Bishop*, and the *Carol Burnett* shows. In the season of 1967-68, he appeared on a total of 25 TV programs, including guest-star appearances on eight segments of *Rowan and Martin's Laugh-In*. From rags, Flip had finally reached riches.

All this was keeping Flip very busy. Besides his TV appearances, he was filling personal engagements throughout the country. Of course, this was nothing new for him. But now, instead of hitchhiking in search of work at small and obscure clubs, he was jetting between engagements at such entertainment meccas as the Rainbow Grill, in New York, and Caesar's Palace, in Las Vegas. He also began making best-selling records and was booked to appear on such TV "specials" as one made by Perry Como.

While this busy schedule was making Flip a wealthy man, his marriage of ten years was becoming emotionally bankrupt. In 1967 Flip and his wife, who was born in the Bahamas, were divorced. Flip has managed to maintain such a wall of privacy around his luckless marriage that few are aware that he's been married and is the father of four children, two boys and two girls.

His former wife lives in Miami and his children visit him whenever possible. For a time, though, this was difficult, since Flip was almost always moving from place to place. "I've been living out of a suitcase for years now," he once said. "My home is whatever hotel I'm staying at. It seems that most of the time I'm living in the friendly skies of United."

The traveling, the rehearsals, the taping of shows, the cutting of records, and the personal appearances often wear Flip out. "Yeah, I get tired," he admits, "but you've got to get it when you can in this business."

"Geraldine" shows her form as a go-go dancer, at left. At right, top to bottom, Flip with guests Gina Lollobrigida and Lena Horne.

"Let's go for broke!" the TV
executive said after seeing Flip on the screen.

XI.

FLIP'S RISE
TO "SUPERSTAR"

To "get it when you can" is an axiom of show business religiously followed by all but the most foolhardy entertainers. In the entertainment world you "get it when you can" because—who knows?—in a few weeks the jobs may get fewer and smaller.

Television is especially notorious for burning out, or at least discarding, talent. It's one thing to have a face that's familiar to TV audiences. It's quite another thing to have a face that audiences have become tired of—or which TV executives *think* the audiences have become tired of. To the star involved, it amounts to the same thing. Just ask Jackie Gleason, or Red Skelton.

As things happily turned out, Flip had no basis in fact for any anxiety he may have felt in the year 1969. But, on the surface, there were enough big decisions being made—and reversed—concerning his fate to give nightmares, ulcers, or at least Excedrin headaches to less philosophical entertainers. It seems that the people who were busy molding his

TV career couldn't decide exactly what to do with Flip.

The big decision began one night when Flip was appearing at the Greek Theater, in Los Angeles. In the audience were two executives from the National Broadcasting Company: Herb Schlosser, the network's West Coast programing executive, and NBC's vice-president, Mort Werner. As Schlosser recalls that night:

"When Flip ran out and just grinned, he lit up the stage, he lit up the audience—he lit up that whole outdoor theater. Besides, he was very funny. That's when we decided to build him up with a lot of guest appearances and by filling in for Johnny Carson. Things like that."

Schlosser describes Flip's sway over audiences as his "likeability factor." When the network executives decided that audiences still liked Flip after numerous appearances on their living-room screens, they decided to take the next step.

"We gave Flip a crack at doing his own 'special,'" Schlosser said. "What a smash *that* was. He grabbed 42 per cent of the audience and was No. 8 in the ratings for that whole week."

When Flip signed his first contract with NBC, he reportedly was to receive $40,000 for each special. But his future, despite the "smash" ratings of his specials, was still far from certain. In fact, he narrowly missed being placed in a show that just could have been a disaster.

"We'd decided to give Flip his own show," said Schlosser, "but we were afraid of tackling all that variety-hour competition with him. Instead, we came up with a little half-hour situation comedy in which Flip would play a talk-show star on a local TV station.

"We took a look at it, then we looked at Flip, then we looked at each other. 'To heck with it,' we said. 'Let's go for broke with a Flip Wilson variety show.'"

As Schlosser indicated, NBC knew it was taking a gamble by putting another variety program on the air. And when you speak of gambling in the television industry, you're talking about a "game" in which the stakes are in the millions of dollars. Werner has been quoted as saying that the network spent a million dollars on pilots and specials for Flip—none of which were even broadcast. Werner reportedly called one special "the worst I've ever seen." He liked one pilot—a sort of trial balloon for a new series—better. He said it was merely "bad."

The fact that Flip's show succeeded despite its variety-show format may be credited in large measure to Bob Henry. It's all too obvious that if you took Flip from the show, the remainder would be just another *Hollywood Palace* —if that. It's not quite so obvious that if you took away Bob Henry, you'd still be left with a possible "flop."

As the producer, Henry is the man responsible for all the aspects of putting the show together each week. He describes his own job this way: "A good producer—a knowing, responsible producer—bears the entire responsibility for the show in all its phases: its budget, costumes, material, songs— everything. A producer hires the director and everybody else on the staff, including the guest stars."

Henry was trying to take no credit whatsoever from Flip, whom he's admired tremendously for

Flip introduces singer Bing Crosby to his audience. Bing—as with many top entertainers who've appeared on Flip's show—needed no "intro" to TV fans. But both seemed to enjoy it, as did the fans.

years. But Henry's job freed Flip from hundreds of details that it would be impossible for him to take care of—and still have any time left to be funny.

"I've never worked so hard on a series in my life. I'm in here at the office at an average of 10 a.m. and go home at 7 or 7:30. I have dinner and watch TV, if anything of professional interest is on, some show I think I should see. Then I get on the phone with the head writer and we do a little refining of the material. I do all this happily, you understand. It's exciting."

58

Henry's excitement was understandable. For a long time he'd tried to do a show starring Flip—but something had always happened to prevent it. "I'd been doing specials for two years," Henry went on, "and for two years I had tried to get Flip on them. But it would always turn out that he was going to be on the *Ed Sullivan Show* or something. Things just never worked out. It became a joke. We were both represented by the same agency yet couldn't get together on a single show. He began to feel like a sought-after bride and I a suitor."

Henry's admiration of Flip probably has absolutely nothing to do with it—but he *looks* somewhat like a white version of Flip Wilson, certainly as far as size is concerned; and his voice, like Flip's, is a gentle one.

Henry tried to describe just why he was so eager, as "a suitor," to get Flip on one of his shows. "Flip has a special appeal on the tube," the producer said. "He's intimate. He has a special quality. For instance, Bob Hope walks out on the stage and says, 'Hi,' and people laugh. Flip, in his own way, has that certain quality. Anyway, I thought he would be great."

After two years of frustration, trying to get Flip on just one of his specials —"wonder of wonders!" as Henry put it. "When NBC felt that Flip should star in his one-hour special, which was really an on-the-air pilot, somehow our agents and NBC got together and decided that I'd be right for him."

Until that point, Henry hadn't even *met* Flip. The first meeting was an unusual interview. Flip was on a table, dressed in a towel and getting a rubdown.

Flip presents Ed Sullivan an "Emmy" at television awards ceremony.

XII.

NO. 1

The meeting between Bob Henry and Flip Wilson took place in the men's locker room near the swimming pool of a hotel just off Sunset Boulevard in Hollywood. As Flip lay there, letting the massager work the kinks out of his back, Henry stroked his own chin, trying to think of a way to persuade a man he'd never met, just why, artistically speaking, they were "meant for each other." Asked about the encounter, Henry replied: "What *could* I say at a first meeting? I told him what I thought of his performances. Then I said to him, with my own candor, I guess, 'If I could *ad lib* a show for you right now, it would show I'm either a creative genius or I'm faking you out.' I guess he appreciated the honesty. Anyway, it was a short meeting. Flip was very serious and made no attempt at humor. But obviously the vibes were right. We began working together at last."

Though he didn't go into much detail at that first meeting, Henry had his own ideas for the show. "I always felt that TV was borrowing too much from Broadway and the movies," he said. "We needed a property intended for a 21-inch tube. It's a *small* tube. If you clutter it up with a lot of people, you lose the most interesting thing in the world—the human face. I wanted to keep things simple. And to achieve simplicity, you have to work twice as hard. We show, basically, Flip and one or two other people—and that's it. We have a minimum of extras or character actors. We rarely exceed three people in a sketch. We do even less music than we did before. But when you put two people on in one six-minute sketch—why, it's really got to be strong stuff to stand up."

When Schlosser had mentioned NBC's decision to "go" with what basically is a streamlined variety show starring Flip Wilson, he'd said it was made "at the last minute, and we haven't regretted it." Surely that must be a rare understatement in a town that's famous for its hyperbole. Throughout its first season, Flip's show traded with *Marcus Welby* for the lead as No. 1 program, which means that according to the Nielsen ratings, more people watched it than any other show.

Long before the first season was over—and long before the network had bothered to give new contracts to some of its other big stars—NBC executives rushed a renewed contract to Flip. And small wonder. Aside from the ratings, the success of the show is spelled out in terms which TV moguls understand even better—money. When Flip's show first went on the air, NBC reportedly sold commercials on it at the rate of $46,000 a minute. After the ratings were released, the price jumped to $55,000. By October, it had risen to $60,000, and the following month to $65,000.

How financially "strong" the show is was demonstrated by the way it weathered a major TV storm. In January 1971 the whole TV industry was dealt a severe financial blow. The Federal Communications Commission had banned cigarette commercials from the airwaves, which meant that the networks would lose millions of dollars in advertising. Partially to fill up this "ad gap," NBC began selling commercials on the basis of a half-minute instead of 60 seconds, hoping to attract advertisers who were on a lower budget than the "cigarette men" had been. At the same time, almost every show decreased the cost of commercials because of poor economic conditions in general.

But none of this seemed to create any financial disturbance on Flip's show. Quite the reverse. It appeared to be a "safe" haven during these times of economic disturbance—and the "admission price" for admen was raised accordingly. Now, instead of asking $65,000 a minute for commercials on this show, the network upped the price to $40,000 for a *half* minute—a mind-spinning rate of $80,000 a minute!

While all this was going on, Flip had his own thoughts. "I worked 15 hard years to become an 'overnight success,'" he reflected.

With a natural smile like that, who needs to say "cheese"?

XIII.

FLIP AND THE ROLLS ROYCE

Soon after it became obvious that Flip would be working full-time in television, he rented a large brick and clapboard house that would have looked more at home in New England than in the hazy hills of Hollywood. The style of architecture didn't matter, however. The significant thing was that, perhaps for the first time in his life, Flip had a place he could consider "home." No more living out of suitcases, no more forwarding addresses, no more need to wander—for the time being, at least.

It may also be significant that, though he could well afford to buy almost any mansion he chose, he decided, instead, to *lease* one said to belong to singer Billy Daniels. Did Flip still distrust his tremendous fortune? Or was it that, finally reaching the pinnacle of success in his field, he simply found no immediate and compelling reason to "sink roots" by building a house? Had he lived "out of a suitcase" too long to take such a drastic step so soon?

Whatever the answers, Flip quickly bought:

—An English bulldog, which he named Geraldine. (He chose what many consider to be an "ugly" breed of dog to teach his children that an ugly exterior can harbor a beautiful soul.)

—A pair of goldfish. (Such domestic touches help to make even a place that doesn't financially belong to you *belong* to you.)

—A dark blue Rolls Royce. (All things considered, the Rolls may have been Flip's wisest, though by no means least expensive, "investment." Flip's use of it sometimes appears to be therapeutic.)

Like most of today's Hollywood stars, Flip has no chauffeur, though in yesteryear it would have been unthinkable for a performer making his kind of money to drive himself anywhere. Flip, who's indicated that he wouldn't particularly care to park cars for a living, likes to drive. But he has such a need for privacy that, even if he hated to be behind the wheel, it seems unlikely that he'd want to share his solitude very often—even with a chauffeur. He uses the car on occasion to *get away* from people.

To appreciate fully one instance in which Flip used the Rolls as "therapy," you must understand where comic material for his TV show comes from and how it's put together. When Flip was assigned his own show, he was also assigned six writers. Now Flip had been writing all his own material for years. As inventive as he is, he certainly didn't rebel at the idea of working with other writers. He realized that the weekly demands for new jokes and situations are far too great for any man to fill, no matter how funny he is.

The show's producer, Henry, told me how he assembled Flip's writing crew. "I'd worked on and off with Herbie Baker over the years," Henry said. "He was an automatic shoo-in to be head writer. Then I got two other good joke writers, who'd written for Lucille Ball and others. All these writers are 45 years old, or older. They've been around. My theory was that if we took their veteran comedy-writing talents and put them together with Flip's glib freshness, we'd have the best. The other writers are younger fellows. Flip takes all the solid material these writers come up with and puts a layer of 'Flip' on it."

Asked if there had ever been a personality clash between Flip and his writers, in view of the fact that so many egos were involved, Henry said, "No, because they "(the writers)" have such mutual respect for each other. Normally, writers are very hesitant when a star shares the credit with them for the writing. But everyone respected Flip's talent right from the start. All those hilarious monologues over the years have been purely Flip, after all; and the other writers knew this about him."

Though he seems to have adjusted remarkably well to TV's system of "comedy by committee," Flip obviously still feels that the primary responsibility for making the show funny is his alone. After all, it's his show. Comedy writers can come and go—as, indeed, at least two on Flip's show already have. One came, and one went. A good comedy writer can quickly find other work in television, so great is the demand for his talents. But when a star loses his show, it's often years—if ever—before he regains a similar "showcase." So, one weekend when Flip was concerned about the writing on the show, he didn't summon a "board meeting" of his writers. He slipped behind the wheel of his Rolls Royce and

Flip obviously doesn't think much of the pool-shooting ability of his guest, Tim Conway. And Conway obviously doesn't think much of Flip's unasked-for advice. Maybe Conway feels he's being "conned."

tooled it along the Freeway and out of the city. The next thing you know, Flip is sitting there, looking at the Grand Canyon, more than 350 miles from Hollywood.

And what was Flip thinking as he gazed at the multicolored sandstone of this natural trench, broad and wide enough to inspire awe in any man? Well, the question that kept running through his mind, he later confessed, was: "What color is the blues?"

Here's how a comic genius works: From that rather philosophical question, Flip's mind somehow jumped the tracks, or leaped in a free fall of fancy, or maybe just stepped through that magic looking glass again. Anyway, he started scribbling furiously in his notebook: "The Negro didn't give the blues to America. America gave the blues to the Negro!"

By the time Flip had driven back to Hollywood and appeared at the writers' meeting in Henry's office the next day, he was happily bubbling with new ideas. "There's this gunfighter named Black Bart, see, and he comes into this town, not knowing that it's segregated," Flip said, rolling his eyes at the writers to make sure they got the picture. "Black Bart's hungry, so he finds this Chinese restaurant, but he has to go around to the back. A guy comes to the window and Black Bart says, 'Chow mein for myself and egg fooyong for my horse.'

"It ends with a duel. The whole town's waiting. Colored and whites on different sides of the street. Blackbirds on one side of the street and doves on the other side of the street. It's a high-noon gun duel. The heavy says to Black Bart, 'I'm gonna shoot when I count to three.'

" Black Bart shoots on the number two. The heavy falls down and complains. Black Bart says, 'You were going to shoot ON THREE.' "

Flip's writers were laughing so hard by this time that their faces were almost cracking. The "boss" was back "with it," hitting on all cylinders. The Rolls Royce had worked its "magic" again.

Flip is so fond of the Rolls that he's given it a name: "Killer"—named after Geraldine's mythical boyfriend.

"Broadway Joe" Namath, New York Jets quarterback, sees how a master comedian "calls the plays." But if he wants to prolong his career with the Jets, he'd better ignore Flip's "chalk-talk" on blackboard.

XIV.

THE BOY WHO COULDN'T PLAY "CHOPSTICKS"

Only a few years ago, TV executives were still in a quandary about producing shows starring blacks. On one hand, they were being pressured to abolish an unwritten rule of the industry that a program starring a black just wouldn't "sell" to predominantly white audiences. On the other, these moguls— none of whom had been accused of racial prejudice in their private lives—were realistic businessmen. If they broke the rule and such a program failed, their own jobs might be endangered.

Then, in an experiment considered bold in those days, the industry learned a new axiom: A program like *I Spy*, which *costarred* a black (in this case, Bill Cosby) could "slip past" the rule. But was the TV audience yet ready for a fine performer like Cosby to star in his own show without a white Robert Culp to give the program a racial "balance"?

Such questions now seem rather quaint in retrospect. At least two series starring blacks, *Julia*

71

and *The Bill Cosby Show*, had done well in the ratings even before Flip's own show was aired, while *The Leslie Uggams Show* proved that a new series starring a black didn't necessarily and always succeed. It now became apparent to the "kingmakers" that TV programing involving blacks wasn't much different from the problem when it involved whites. The trick was still to find a show that would catch on with audiences, whether a black or a white was the star. This would seem to indicate one of two things: Maybe the early forerunners of "integrated" shows had quickly done much to overcome the racial prejudice of TV viewers. Or could it be that the viewers hadn't been as prejudiced as they'd been accused of being in the first place?

In any case, Flip's tremendous popularity, with a few notable exceptions, cuts across both regional and racial boundaries. He's a favorite with viewers, not only in the larger cities, but in the Midwest and South. An interesting, and ironic, aspect of his popularity is that his most outspoken critics aren't to be found among his white audiences but among his fellow blacks.

Black militants have criticized him for being "a handkerchief head"—a term connoting a shuffle-foot kind of humor subservient to whites. It could be, however, that anyone who accuses Flip of undue "humility" in his humor either is humorless himself or too overly sensitive about the whole subject of race to get Flip's "message."

For example, in a recent TV skit with Don Rickles, Flip played the part of a street urchin, dressed outlandishly in a pink bonnet, a baggy sweater, knickers, and tennis shoes. Rickles, white-wigged

and otherwise made up as a rich old man, catches
Flip trying to steal his shoes. For some insane reason, the old man decides, instead of calling the police, to teach the urchin to play the piano.

Rickles is a hard taskmaster. Every time Flip
misses a note while trying to play "Chopsticks"—
and he makes so many mistakes it's obvious the kid
will *never* master this "classic"—Rickles rewards
him for the effort by whacking him over the hands
with a ruler.

The rulers used here were "breakaway" props.
Every time Rickles slapped one over Flip's hands,
pieces of wood went flying everywhere. Rickles
would then calmly select another ruler from a huge
pile stacked on the piano, just in time for Flip to
make another "mistake." *Whack* would go the
ruler. More pieces of wood would fly. Soon the
whole stage is almost ankle-deep in splinters. Finally, Rickles gets a little too enthusiastic and "breaks"
Flip's fingers.

Now, so far it's easy to see how this scene might
irritate a black extremist if he's humorless enough to
take it seriously. He could argue that it's degrading
to his race to see a poor little black boy being "exploited" by a rich "whitey" and that the whole
"flogging scene" is too reminiscent of the mistreat-
ment of black slaves in days of yore to be funny.

Raising such an objection is certainly the critic's
privilege. There's no law saying that you have to
think Flip is funny. But if one insists on taking such
slapstick seriously enough to subject it to critical
analysis, we would instead say, "Right on!" For
could such a critic ignore the rest of the "message" in the skit? This bit with Rickles ends when

73

Flip discovers that, still unable to play "Chop-sticks" with two uninjured fingers, now with ten broken ones he can play the beautiful, rolling passages of Chopin and Mozart. The waif has *overcome* the disadvantages. Right? *Who's* exploited now? The young pianist's skills are so great that the King arrives to hear him play!

Flip and his writers seem far too busy having *fun* to give conscious thought as to what serious interpretation might be given such skits. The point is, though, that if someone does insist on being serious, and not just angry, in analyzing Flip's artistry, he should make sure to hear the man through. To get *all* the "message."

What seems to annoy Flip's black critics consistently, more than anything else, is his character "Geraldine Jones." An article *Ebony* magazine recently published on "The Evolution of Geraldine" drew a number of letters from readers, some of them irate. One wrote, "This Geraldine character is especially repulsive and degrading. The black woman has, for too long, been stripped of her femininity and beauty by a racist society. Flip Wilson is obviously making it so big so quick because he is doing exactly what the white world wants him to do: continue to sell out our people for a couple of coins."

But, since other letter writers praised Flip (one termed him "a brilliant intellectual"), it mainly shows that, to some extent, Flip is somewhat controversial. Almost anyone who creates a stir is. While some see Geraldine as a put down of Negro womanhood, others see her as a satire on the female "mystique" in general. They say the fact that

Geraldine is black is incidental; Flip just happens to be black, too. And the fact that she's obviously somewhat shy of formal education certainly casts no slur. Few white women—educated or uneducated—could match wits with Geraldine.

Perhaps John Leonard, a TV critic, touched on the thing that bothers Flip's black antagonists the most. Writing in a recent issue of *Life* magazine, he said: "What Flip Wilson has accomplished is almost incredible in a time of Black Panthers and savage rhetoric. He has taken the *threat* out of the fact of blackness. He wouldn't hurt you, any more than Glen Campbell or Carol Burnett or Ed Sullivan would hurt you. Or Captain Kangaroo." Perhaps it is Flip's mildness—the lack of threat—that bothers some black militants.

Any controversy generated by Geraldine or any of his other characters leaves Flip outwardly undisturbed. He seems to scoff, though mildly, at those who object to another Wilsonian character, "Reverend Leroy." The Reverend, a sort of black Elmer Gantry, is obviously something besides a man of the cloth. He's a "con artist" interested in things other than the souls of those who attend his "The Church of What's Happening Now."

"Every black person has known a Reverend Leroy," Flip said. "I met mine when I was 9 and I was the best testifier in our little church."

When Flip is asked what his attitude is toward racial humor in general, he says:

"I don't steer away from it. The main thing is to make sure it's in good taste."

Then, with a smile, he adds : "Why, some of my best friends are colored people!"

During an "airline flight" on show, "Geraldine," the air stewardess, was intent on winning million-dollar bonus for friendly service to airline customers and befriends jet-age "granny" (Jonathan Winters).

XV.

FLIP AND THE
"IMAGE-MAKERS"

Flip Wilson in Hollywood is quite a different person from the Flip Wilson in New York, Las Vegas, or wherever else he might have been staying briefly less than three years ago. This change hasn't helped his journalistic image.

Actually, it's not that Flip has changed so much as his status has undergone drastic revision. Now that he's a big star, he's sought by a multitude of such "image-makers" as writers and photographers from magazines and newspapers. Just a few years ago, it was relatively easy for almost any writer to get permission to interview Flip. Today, all that has changed. Under the pressure of putting out a TV show each week, Flip soon discovered that he simply didn't have time enough to see every "image-maker" who wanted to see him. He would have to be highly selective in granting their requests.

There are some who would say that "selective" is hardly the word. Today, Flip apparently thinks nothing of turning away writers who are used to interviewing such major and longtime stars as Bob Hope, Bill Cosby, Carol Burnett, and Andy Williams. On at least one occasion he's refused an interview with a journalist who had interviewed two Presidents of the United States.

The problem for writers these days is to get close enough to Flip to see whether he'll talk to them or not. With his passion for privacy, Flip is now surrounded by a "security system" resembling a series of old-fashioned Chinese boxes; boxes within boxes.

The bigger boxes are the NBC-TV building and Flip's secret "hideaway," his home high in the Hollywood hills. Take his house, for instance. Hollywood is so publicity-oriented that any tourist can, for a dollar, pick up from the counter of hundreds of drugstores or souvenir shops a map designating "the homes of the stars." But he could go blind looking for the "X" marking Flip's house. It simply isn't there. Why?

Just ask the man on the sightseeing bus. That's the one that drives past these houses, ever so slowly, so that when the uniformed guide says, "Now, ladies and gentlemen, to our left we have..." everyone has equal opportunity to s t r e t c h his neck, like a giraffe, in an effort to see *over* the wall, and not just look *at* it.

"Where's Flip Wilson's place?" you might ask the man. And he'd have to admit that even those who make a *business* of finding out such things still just don't know.

Or, take Flip's "office." That's his dressing-room suite in the big green-and-white box of a building which contains the NBC-TV studios. This box is surrounded by a high wire fence, locked gates, and uniformed guards who challenge anyone who comes within 20 paces.

The shades to this building aren't drawn; but this could hardly be regarded as a security gap, since the building rises three stories above a neighborhood of modest bungalows. In fact, many of the bungalows have *their* shades drawn, whether against the sight of distant, smog-veiled mountains—or against the NBC building—it's hard to say. In any case, the secrecy seems to be catching; and Flip's outer security box has something going for it both ways.

Inside the largest Chinese box—the NBC building—is the second biggest box. It's marked "press department." It's protected not only by that high wire fence and the uniformed guards outside; inside, it fends off much of the verbal world by a very efficient crew of telephone operators. If any "image-maker's" story is legit, he *might* get to somebody's secretary. But it had better be good; and, from then on, things get tougher.

Whatever the journalist's pitch is, though, if he's trying to get to Flip chances are he won't get past this second box. Say, for example, he had a *compelling* reason. Suppose he wanted to tell Flip that his house was on fire. He'd first have to talk to Monte Kay. And that's a job in itself. Kay represents the third Chinese box. And on more than one occasion he's proven to be almost as elusive to inquiring reporters as Flip himself.

The smallest, most interior, most "secret" box of all, of course, is reserved for Flip himself. When he retreats into this box, apparently *no one* can reach him, maybe not even Monte Kay. Who knows?

Henry, Flip's producer who telephones the head writer almost every night, said he had talked to Flip on the phone "two or three times" during the entire four months that the program had been on the air. Of course that could be because Henry didn't want to bother Flip; but, it could be because Henry didn't know Flip's telephone number.

All this privacy—or secrecy, if you will—on Flip's part has led to what some press agents would consider to be disastrous public relations. Hollywood reporters are still chortling over the experience that *Life* magazine underwent when it recently tried to do a big spread on Flip. The magazine sent one of its top writers to do an "in-depth" piece on TV's brightest young comedian. Flip agreed. The writer soon learned that his idea of privacy and Flip's definition of the word just didn't agree. As one member of the Hollywood press corps put it: "Man, this guy from *Life* would say, 'Hello, Flip. What did you do last night?' 'That's a personal question,' Flip would say. You know, he wouldn't even say, 'I slept for eight hours.' So the writer says, 'Sorry about that. By the way, can we take some pictures of you at your house?' And Flip says, 'It's my time to be sorry. I just can't allow it.' And so on. It went like that for three days. Finally, the writer told his office, 'Look, there's just no *story* here!' So they dropped plans for the whole article."

Even on the few occasions when Flip has co-operated with writers, his growing hostility toward "personal" publicity often has been reinforced by what he regards as their unfair or inconsiderate treatment of him. Flip has admitted that he was quite upset by a recent interview involving a "big name" magazine free-lancer, a veteran of his craft. Flip agreed to an interview with him—and when the story was published Flip was furious. The story failed to use a single quote from the interview! It was all about the writer's *impressions* of Flip. Though these seemed complimentary enough, Flip's attitude was: "Here I've given this man a lot of my time, and all he uses is stuff he could get from old newspaper clippings. Why bother?"

A friend of Flip confided: "I think Flip was also upset by a couple of other little touches. For instance the story referred to his former wife as 'a Bahamian woman.' How gauche can you get! The phrase makes her sound as though she goes around carrying a bunch of bananas on her head!"

Nature abhors a vacuum; so does any Hollywood writer. The mystery surrounding Flip's private life has led many journalists to engage in guessing games, which is fair enough. But many of these games have ended up as printed "fact." For example, one recent magazine story pictured Flip as leading a "lonely" life offstage.

"Contented" would have been a better word. It's true that Flip seldom feels an urge to go out at night. Why should he care for Hollywood night life? After all, he's already spent much of his life working in nightclubs. Flip likes to escape the "rat race" of stage life occasionally by playing a quiet game of pool or a hand of cards with his secretary, George Whittington, who used to be with the Modern Jazz Quartet. But only a jaded journalist who equates "the good life" with "night life" would picture Flip as "lonely." Now and then he holds a rap session with some show-business friend, like Arte Johnson.

The table was turned when TV-interviewer David Frost appeared on Flip's show—and found himself being interviewed by a "short-order cook" who's better at "grilling" customers than in using the kitchen grill.

(It's difficult to imagine an evening as being "lonely" with this talented *Laugh-In* clown around to liven things up.) Flip is occasionally visited by his children. And sometimes he dates. (Just who, of course, is another mystery.) But mostly Flip works. Not because he *has* to; but because he *wants* to. He worked hard to get on top. Is it surprising that he works hard to stay on top?

The high value Flip places on his privacy is calculated to make neither journalists nor their friends in NBC-TV's public relations department happy. The latter's job is theoretically to "feed" information on stars such as Flip to the press. But PR men can distinguish between butter and bread; so instead of seeing that Flip Wilson gets as much public "exposure" as possible, they *protect* Flip from the public as much as possible, since he wants it that way. And it's a good thing they agree with Flip's aims, since his "Chinese boxes" insulate him rather heavily even against his own PR men. Apparently, Flip feels that he's in show business not politics, and what he does offstage is simply no one's business but his own. All he owes the public is to give it the best of himself when he's *on* stage. And, to do that, he has to stick by his own rules.

As for whether he's "lonely" or otherwise unhappy in his private moments, Flip smiles and says in that soft voice of his: "I dreamed it all. I got the cookie in the dream."

The 31st George Foster Peabody Awards went to (left to right) the Very Rev. Michael Kennedy, head of Loyola University; Theodor Geisel, better known as "Dr. Seuss," and to Cleon—better known as Flip.

XVI.

AN EVENING WITH FLIP AND FRIENDS

If he could read English, even a visitor from Outer Mongolia could guess the star's name as soon as he stepped into the studio where Flip's show is videotaped each week. Serving as backdrop to the stage are walls on which is inscribed a modernistic design. Upon looking closer, though, you see that the design spells:

FLIP FLIP FLIP FLIP FLIP FLIP

The design isn't all that obvious, though, because interspersed with the plainly spelled-out FLIPs are cases in which the name appears as ꟼILꟻ as well as ꟻIⱵꟼ. It seemed obvious that, design-wise, Flip's Air Force buddies had done him a real favor when they gave him the name Flip.

The show about to be taped was a very funny one. But before it began, the live audience was almost murdered by an ancient studio gimmick dating back to "the golden age of radio." This age-old device is called "the audience warm-up." More accurately, it could be called "the audience turn-

85

off." An impossibly jolly announcer jumps onto the stage like a Jack-in-the-Box and starts "making friends" with these total strangers:

"Why, hello, there! How are all you good people tonight? Gee, we've got a real great audience here tonight! I can look at you and *tell*! Where are you nice people from? You, sir! Where's your home? *Sausalito*! Isn't that great? (There's a smattering of applause from the Sausalito "delegation.") How many other people are from Sausalito? That's wonderful! Where else are you from? You, miss! Where are you from? *Denver*! My, my! And is that gentleman with you from Denver, too? Oh, he's your *husband*! I thought he might be your *father*! (A slight tittering.) No offense, sir. You *know* I was just kidding…"

And so on it goes. Actually, the announcer is doing a splendid job, accomplishing exactly what the "warm-up" is psychologically designed to do: bore the audience silly. Boy, will it ever be glad to see Flip *now*! Soon the victims are ready for the final stage of the "warm-up." That begins when the announcer says, "You know, we've got such a great crowd here tonight, we'd better test your reactions on our sound equipment. We wouldn't want to blow any tubes back there, would we? For our engineers, will you give us a big round of applause, so they can check their instruments?"

By now, many in the audience—particularly those who haven't been able to tell the announcer where *they*'re from—are happy to participate in this seance in any way possible. So when the announcer asks them to applaud, and for no other reason, they… just… *applaud*.

"That's fine," says the maestro. "But I'm not sure your heart was really in that one. I'll bet some of you guys out there can whistle, too—*right*? Let's try it again!"

After a few prods like that, the audience is in this thing *together*. It's like a game at your seventh birthday party. Only now, you don't try to break a balloon to win a prize. Instead, the object is to break the sound engineer's instruments. Though a number in the audience suspect that this really can't be done by applause alone (and they're right; it can't), they try anyway.

As soon as the audience is "warmed up" to the announcer's satisfaction, he disappears from the stage and is immediately followed by—Flip!

He walks down one of the aisles leading to the six-sided, red-carpeted stage. The audience goes wild at the mere sight of him. Whether the "warm-up" has contributed to the volume of applause is anybody's guess. Considering what they've been through, those who've been waiting for Flip may be doubly glad to see him. On the other hand, how much abuse can a pair of palms take, even when they're trying to applaud louder? In any case, the applause is genuine now, and the announcer was right: There *are* some men in the audience who can whistle. And they do.

Flip is a walking testimonial to Carnaby Street. His shirt, tie, and Edwardian suit with its flared jacket are a symphony in brown. He bounces through the door, bounces down the aisle, bounces up the stairs of the stage; he's so full of life he still seems to bounce even when he's just standing there acknowledging the welcome.

"We're going to have a great show tonight," he says. And who could doubt him? For who's to appear with Flip but Don Rickles, television's "Mr. Mirth"; Leslie Uggams, the great singer; and the idol of some of Flip's funniest routines, Ray Charles himself.

If the audience thinks that Flip is going to start cracking it up immediately, though, it's in for a disappointment. First, there's some "business" to attend to. At one point, Flip sits down and, with a TV camera trained on him, says, "Don't go away. We'll be right back." *This* audience isn't about to go away. Things haven't even started happening yet. But these segments of the show obviously will be spliced into the videotape at the proper places; and to do them now, before stagehands start cluttering up the bare stage with scenery, makes logistical sense. In fact, efficiency is the watchword in taping *The Flip Wilson Show*. Later on, there were as many as nine stagehands working simultaneously. Retakes can plague any show; equipment breaks or is improperly adjusted, forcing the performers to go through the scene again. They are a waste of time and money. During this entire evening of taping *The Flip Wilson Show*, there wasn't a single retake.

A lot of this efficiency is reflected by Flip himself. After delivering a monologue or doing a scene, Flip bows a couple of times and—fffttt!—disappears, no matter *how* loud the applause is. After all, if he took any more bows, they would just end up on the traditional cutting-room floor. And Flip seems quite aware that the truism, "time is money," is especially apt when a show is being taped. No one in the audience can rightfully resent it if he becomes aware occasionally that Flip is playing to the cameras instead of his live admirers. After all, that's what the show is all about. The *real* audience isn't the one seated here. The *real* audience is the one "out there" somewhere in videoland, in thousands of places; but wherever it is, it's all focused in a spot behind the lens of a TV camera. It must have required a great deal of discipline for a comedian who'd played to nothing but live audiences for so long to learn to adjust to TV's requirements so quickly. In any case, while watching Flip tape a show, one is likely to get the feeling now and then that comedy can be a serious business. Flip's face is extremely animated when one of the little red lights on the cameras is turned on, a signal that the camera is in use. But as soon as the red lights go out, Flip turns off his face, so to speak. Instead of looking like the comedian we're used to seeing on the TV screen, he sometimes looks like a preoccupied businessman. Which, of course, is what he is: a businessman whose business is to make people laugh. This he certainly does—whenever one of those little red lights is on.

At another extreme, we have Don Rickles. Give Don an audience, and he feels compelled to be funny whether the little red lights are on or not. In fact, sometimes the little red lights *aren't* on simply because Don can't stop ad-libbing one-liners and making jokes that aren't called for in the script. "Hello, sisters," he calls to three Roman Catholic nuns seated in the third row. "Where are you from?" They name a certain nearby Catholic hospital. "Oh?" says Don. "Who's minding the store?" The sisters laugh behind their hands.

When Don is "turned on"—and he certainly is tonight—he seems like a man possessed. His wild grin reminds you of a jack-o'-lantern as he nervously surveys the audience, looking for a target to insult. His art lies in the fact that he can say truly outrageous things to people, yet they come out seeming funny—even to the "victims" themselves. There's a dramatic school known as "The Theater of Cruelty"; and Don's talent certainly must be related to it. Yet, amazingly enough, his biting remarks don't seem cruel. Whatever he says that's mean or petty or biting isn't really the way *he* feels. He's merely *saying* it. Somehow, he's innocent. Many in the world might *think* such contemptible things about other people, and maybe might even feel ashamed for thinking them. Don departs from the norm by coming right out and *saying* them—in a way that leaves you believing he doesn't really think that way at all.

Thus he can even insult children, and it comes out funny. "Can you see all right, kid?" he calls to a boy who, not content to be in the front row, has placed his elbows on the stage which, in that section of the studio, is quite low. "Can you see all right, kid? It looks like you're car sick."

Whether all Don's antics amuse Flip as much as they do the audience is a moot point. But his uninhibited guest unquestionably almost breaks up Flip himself a couple of times. While technicians are making final adjustments for the skit in which Rickles, the white-bearded music teacher, teaches Flip to play classical music by breaking his fingers, Don plucks at Flip's "waif" costume. "Is this your good sweater?" he deadpans.

Flip enjoys that one, remembering perhaps the

times when even such a baggy sweater would have been a welcome addition to his wardrobe. Another "insult" dealt to the show's host strikes Flip as even funnier.

Those nine stagehands have done their magic. They synchronized their watches and staged a split-second "invasion" on the stage. From one direction marched two, carrying a couple of chairs while others set up the "walls" of a living room and still others were parceling out small tables, lamps, and a telephone. Presto! Almost as soon as you can count the stagehands, you're looking at a completely furnished "pad." Flip is in it; he's lonely, and decides to take advantage of a new telephone service— "Dial-A-Friend." Some friend! He turns out to be Don Rickles.

The hired "friend" is highly unpredictable—and highly unionized. While "on duty" he listens sympathetically to Flip's tale of woe. Poor Flip! He's a social wallflower, if you can believe it; Don decides to give him dancing lessons, to build up his self-confidence. In a hilarious scene, Flip and Don do a little old-fashioned, cheek-to-cheek dancing, mugging it up and otherwise dealing no threat to Fred Astaire. Then, just when Flip is glowing with happiness from his newly purchased friendship, Rickles glances at his watch and declares it's time for his 10-minute "break." He spends this time telling the social misfit what he *really* thinks of him. And all these insults are up to the usual Rickles standards. But Flip seems to feel that the best insult of all was an off-camera one. While this scene was still being set up, Rickles glanced around and again sighted "the kid." Still with his elbows on the stage.

Flip shakes hands with David Steinberg—but seems to have eyes only for his teddy bear. As with other comics, Flip and David form a "mutual admiration society:" They don't just "bear" each other.

There was obviously a communication between Don and this boy—"vibes" maybe you'd call it. Anyway, all Don had to do this time was *look* at the boy—and the boy began laughing.

"We just come in here to do a show, and the kid turns purple," Don says.

You could see yourself in those black, shiny shoes of Ray's—if they were still long enough. But

if it's a fast number, his feet are flying in fancy fili-
grees worthy of Bojangles Robinson. So, there's the
problem: In a tennis match, you've got only the one
tennis ball to follow with your eyes. Watching Ray
Charles is like watching a three-ring circus—hands,
feet, smile. It's not always easy, but it's certainly
worth the effort.

There may be some who'd say that Ray Charles is
an *impossible* act to follow. Maybe not even Flip
Wilson could follow him. But Geraldine can, and
does. Well, even that isn't entirely correct. Geraldine doesn't exactly follow Ray, "she" appears on-
stage with him—and the audience obviously thinks
that is some combination. So does Ray Charles. He
is rocking with laughter as soon as Geraldine tries to
go onstage and is loudly intercepted by Don Rickles, now playing the part of an usher.

"Madam, you can't go on stage!" Rickles pro-
tests.

"Don't you touch me!" huffs Geraldine in that
high voice of hers. "Don't you *ever* touch me!"

After quite a few more words—and to no one's
surprise—Geraldine wins. Doesn't she always?

Usually as soon as the show's over, Flip goes immediately to his dressing room. But tonight, a studio
cameraman wants to take some still pictures of Flip
as Geraldine.

Flip's transformation into this delightful character is so complete, it was rather startling to hear the
shrill Geraldine speak in Flip's normal voice. It pro-
duced what must have been a similar effect as when,
years ago, Flip played the part of Clara Barton in his
usual voice. As everyone knows, Geraldine and
Clara Barton are leagues apart both in time and tem-

The boxer, Muhammed Ali (Cassius Clay), looks slightly uncomfortable—and just may wish he were back in the ring. That could be particularly true if "Geraldine" turns belligerent—as she often does.

perament. Yet, in a sense, this female evolution—
from Clara to Geraldine—is the life story of this
brilliantly complex comic genius.

Entertaining TV watchers week after week is a
big job. For years such entertainment has been a
very large part of Flip's life; and he's always been
determined to give the world the very best he's got.
By most standards of comedy, many of us would
agree that's more than plenty.

So, thank *you*, Flip Wilson. Thanks for helping
make videoland —which is part of our world—a
funnier, and nicer, place to be.

Then, quickly, to Flip he adds: "No offense
meant!"

Flip cracks up himself, holding onto Rickles'
shoulder for support. "Why don't you go over and
join the kid?" Don asks. Then, over his shoulder to
his young "volunteer" straight man. "I don't know
who you are, kid. But you're never coming in here
again."

Leslie Uggams slinks onstage next, wearing a
dress of "golden" chains that must weigh about 20
pounds. If she falls, it might be disastrous. Not only
might it take about three stagehands to get her ver-
tical, but the fall might break one of her manicured
nails which, from the front row, appear to be about
three inches long. Silver. Silver nails and gold
chains. But Leslie has something besides a closetful
of attractive clothes. She's got a voice; and does she
use it tonight!

As they say in show biz, Leslie is a hard act to
follow. One of the few entertainers who can ac-
complish that difficult feat, perhaps, is Ray Charles.
When Flip introduces him, there's probably more

than one fan in the audience who's aware of Flip's great regard for this gifted musician and who recalls Flip's now-famous line that if Columbus doesn't discover America, "there ain't going to be any Ray Charles." Tonight, Ray immediately sets out to prove that Columbus' voyage was well worth the trouble.

You can see, maybe, how a fellow with shades over his sightless eyes can play the piano. Others have done it, though maybe not nearly so well. You can also see how a blind man can sing—though, again, maybe not so well as Ray Charles. But this man plays the piano, sings—and *dances*—all at the same time. When you're watching Ray Charles perform, your eyes are busier than they are when you're looking at a tennis match. You feel that you've got to catch the way Ray flashes those big, pearly teeth in a dazzling smile if the song is joyous; or, if it's a blues piece, you've got to watch the way Ray is really crying. You can't see the tears behind those dark glasses; but you can *hear* the tears in his voice; and, what's more, you can *see* them, it seems, in Ray's painful smile. He's still smiling even though his emotions may be *killing* him. Ray's smile is something to watch; and if anyone could somehow resist following the drama of it, he'd be missing a great deal of the Charles performance. At the same time, you've got to be looking at his hands, too. How do those hands hit just the right keys every time? Especially since a lot of the time Ray is bouncing off the piano stool so high you get the idea that maybe he should install a seat belt just for safety's sake. And that reminds you of the dancing feet.